The Best
PARTY SNACKS

The Best
PARTY SNACKS

Dips, Nibbles, Spreads, Kabobs, and Other Festive Fare

By Gregg R. Gillespie

BLACK DOG
& LEVENTHAL
PUBLISHERS
NEW YORK

Published by
Black Dog & Leventhal Publishers, Inc.
151 West 19th Street
New York, NY 10011

Distributed by
Workman Publishing
708 Broadway
New York, NY 10003

Manufactured in Spain

ISBN 1-57912-296-5

Library of Congress Cataloging-in-Publication Data is on file and available
from Black Dog & Leventhal Publishers, Inc.

Cover and interior design by 27.12 Design, Ltd.
Interior layout by Sheila Hart Design, Inc.
Photography by Zeva Oelbaum

g f e d c b a

CONTENTS

ANCHOVY AND BACON WRAPS
Makes 16 rolls

8 strips bacon, cut in half
8 anchovy fillets

Drawn Butter Sauce (recipe follows)

1. Preheat the broiler.
2. Lay an anchovy fillet on each bacon piece and roll each tight. Fasten each with a toothpick and dip in butter sauce. Broil for several minutes, turning at least once, until the bacon is crisp. Serve immediately with the remaining butter.

DRAWN BUTTER SAUCE
Makes 1¾ cups

3 tbsp. unsalted butter plus ¾ tbsp. butter
3 tbsp. all-purpose flour
1½ cups boiling water

In a small saucepan, over medium-low heat, melt the 3 tablespoons of butter. Add the flour, stirring constantly until mixed and smooth. Add the water and cook for 5 minutes, stirring. Add the remaining butter, stir until incorporated and serve immediately.

ANCHOVY-FLAVORED STUFFED EGGS

Makes 8 servings

4 large hard-cooked eggs, cut in half and yolks removed
¼ cup Anchovy Butter (recipe follows)
1 tbsp. minced parsley
Paprika

1. In a small bowl, combine the egg yolks, butter, and parsley. Using a pastry bag fitted with a large fancy tip, press a liberal amount of the filling into each half egg white.
2. Sprinkle with paprika and place on a plate, platter or tray. Chill until ready to serve.

ANCHOVY BUTTER

Makes about ¼ cup

¼ cup unsalted butter
1 tsp. anchovy paste
⅛ tsp. lemon or lime juice

In a small bowl or cup, mash the butter until soft and creamy using a fork. Fold in the anchovy paste and lemon juice, blending thoroughly.

ARTICHOKE NIBBLES

Makes about 40 servings

1 tbsp. canola oil
1 white onion, chopped
1 clove garlic, minced
1 jar (7 oz.) water-packed
   artichoke hearts, drained
   and chopped, liquid reserved

3 large eggs
1 cup grated Cheddar cheese
¼ tsp. dried crushed oregano
Salt and pepper
2 tbsp. dry bread crumbs

1. Position the rack in the center of the oven and preheat to 325 degrees.
   Lightly grease a 9-inch square baking pan.
2. In a large skillet, heat the oil over medium heat and sauté the onions
   and garlic for about 5 minutes until translucent. Add the artichokes
   and stir.
3. In a large bowl, whisk the eggs until foamy and add the onion mixture.
   Add the cheese, reserved liquid from the artichokes and oregano and
   stir well. Season with salt and pepper and transfer to the baking pan.
   Sprinkle with the bread crumbs and bake for 25 to 30 minutes or until
   firm. Cool for about 10 minutes before cutting into small squares.
   Serve warm or cold.

ARTICHOKE SPREAD

Makes 12 to 15 servings

1 jar (6 oz.) marinated
  artichokes
1 cup grated Parmesan cheese

¾ cup mayonnaise
Pumpernickel cocktail bread

In a bowl, mash the artichokes. Add the cheese and mayonnaise and mix well. Spread on the bread.

ASPARAGUS APPETIZERS

Makes 12 to 24 servings

12 oz. asparagus spears, trimmed
1 tbsp. water
2 packages (3 oz. each) cream cheese, at room temperature
1 package (2 oz.) blue cheese, crumbled
1 tsp. lemon juice
Crackers for serving

1. Cut the asparagus spears into 1-inch pieces.
2. In a 2-cup microwave-safe bowl, combine the asparagus and water. Cover with plastic wrap, leaving a corner turned back for venting, or a microwave safe lid and microwave on high (100 percent) power for 4 to 5 minutes, or until tender. Drain.
3. In a bowl, and using an electric mixer on medium speed, beat the cream cheese, blue cheese, and lemon juice until smooth. Spread the cheese mixture on crackers and garnish with the asparagus.

ASPARAGUS-STUFFED
HAM ROLLS
Makes 8 servings

¼ cup mayonnaise
½ tsp. prepared mustard
16 asparagus spears, trimmed

French dressing
16 slices thinly sliced
  smoked ham

1. In a cup, combine the mayonnaise and mustard and chill.
2. Place the asparagus in a shallow bowl and spoon enough French dressing over to cover. Cover and chill for 4 hours.
3. Lay the smoked ham on a work surface and spread an even layer of the mayonnaise-mustard mixture on each slice. Lay an asparagus spear on each slice of ham and roll into a tight roll. Chill for 1 hour before serving. Serve the rolls with the mustard dressing on the side.

BACON-WRAPPED SHRIMP

Makes 6 servings

2 pounds jumbo shrimp, peeled and deveined
3 tbsp. red wine vinegar
3 tbsp. canola oil
1 clove garlic, mashed
1 tsp. snipped fresh oregano
¼ tsp. garlic powder

1 tbsp. chopped fresh parsley
1 red onion, sliced
Salt and pepper
15 to 18 strips bacon, cut in half (depending on number of shrimp)

1. In a large bowl, combine all of the ingredients except the bacon. Cover and chill for 8 to 12 hours. Remove the shrimp and set aside. Pour the liquid into a small saucepan.
2. Over medium-low heat, cook the liquid until reduced to about 1 cup.
3. Position the broiler rack 6 inches from the heat and preheat the broiler. Lightly grease a broiler tray.
4. Wrap each shrimp with ½ a strip of bacon and lay on the tray, seasoning each with salt and pepper before rolling up. Broil for 3 to 4 minutes or until the bacon is crisp. Serve with sauce in a dipping cup alongside.

BACON-AND-CHEESE FINGERS

Makes about 30 servings

1 cup shredded Swiss or
  Muenster cheese
8 slices crisp bacon, crumbled
3 to 3¼ cups mayonnaise

1 tbsp. grated shallot
¼ tsp. celery salt
10 slices white bread, crusts
  removed and cut into thirds

1. Position the rack in the center of the oven and preheat to 325 degrees. Lightly grease a baking sheet.
2. In a medium bowl, combine the cheese, bacon, mayonnaise, shallot, and celery salt and blend with a fork. Spread evenly to the very edge of the bread slices and place on the baking sheet. Bake for 8 to 10 minutes, or until the cheese melts, and serve immediately.

BAKED
SCALLOPS

Makes 40 servings

2 garlic cloves, minced
2 tbsp. butter or margarine,
   at room temperature
8 oz. cooked scallops, chopped
½ cup grated Cheddar
   or Colby cheese

⅛ tsp. Worcestershire sauce
Salt and pepper
2 packages (11 oz. each) pie
   crust mix

1. Position the rack in the center of the oven and preheat to 450
   degrees. Lightly grease 2 baking sheets.
2. In a skillet over medium heat, sauté the garlic in the butter for 1 to 2
   minutes, or until soft. Remove from the heat and stir in the remaining
   ingredients except the pie crust mix.
3. Prepare the pie crust according to the package directions and roll out
   to ⅛- to ¼ -inch thick. Using a round or scalloped cookie cutter, cut
   into 2-inch circles.
4. Using a pastry brush, moisten the edges of the party circles with
   water, place 1 teaspoon of the scallop mix in the center, and top with
   another circle, pressing the edges together to seal securely. Prick the
   tops with a fork and place on the prepared baking sheets about 1
   inch apart.
5. Bake for 8 to 10 minutes, or until light golden brown. Transfer to wire
   rack to cool slightly before serving.

BAÑDERILLAS

Makes about 20 servings

1 pound cooked medium, shelled shrimp

2 cans (14 oz. each) water-packed artichoke hearts, drained and halved

¾ cup Italian dressing

¼ cup finely chopped cilantro

1. In a bowl, combine the shrimp, artichoke hearts, dressing, and cilantro and stir gently to mix. Cover and chill for at least 8 hours, stirring occasionally.
2. Thread the shrimp and artichokes, alternating each, onto 4-inch toothpicks.

BEEF
EMPANADAS
Makes about 18 servings

16 oz. lean ground beef
1 small shallot, chopped
1 potato, finely chopped
1 can (8.5 oz.) mixed peas and
  carrots, drained

1 package (1 oz.) mushroom
  gravy mix
1 cup water
1 package (22 oz.) pie crust mix
Paprika

1. In a nonstick skillet, combine the beef and shallot and cook for 7 to 8
   minutes over medium heat, stirring, until the beef is browned. Drain
   the fat. Add the potato, peas and carrots, gravy mix, and water and
   stir to blend. Raise the heat and bring to a boil. Reduce the heat and
   simmer for 2 to 4 minutes, or until the liquid is reduced by half.
2. Position the rack in the center of the oven and preheat to 400 degrees.
3. Prepare the pie crust mix according to the package directions and roll
   out. Using a 3-inch biscuit cutter or upturned glass, stamp out about
   18 rounds. Lay them on an ungreased baking sheet, leaving about 1
   inch between them. Spoon a tablespoonful of the beef mixture over
   half of each round and then fold the pastry over the filling. Crimp the
   edges closed with the tines of a fork. Sprinkle with paprika and bake
   for 12 to 15 minutes or until the pastry is golden brown. Serve warm.

BEER-BATTER FRANKS

Makes 24 servings

sauce
⅓ to ½ cup dry mustard
½ cup distilled white vinegar
½ cup sugar
1 large egg yolk

frankfurters
¾ cup all-purpose flour
½ cup flat beer
1 tbsp. canola oil
1 large egg white
Oil for frying
24 cocktail franks

1. To make the sauce, in a small bowl, whisk the mustard and vinegar together. Cover and let stand at room temperature for at least 8 hours or overnight.
2. In a small saucepan, combine the mustard mixture, sugar, and egg yolk and whisk well. Bring to a simmer over low heat and cool until thickened to the consistency of salad dressing. Cover and chill until ready to use. (Makes about 1⅓ cups.)
3. To prepare the franks, in a small bowl, using an electric mixer on medium speed, beat together the flour, beer, and canola oil.
4. In a small bowl, using an electric mixer, beat the egg white until stiff but not dry. Fold into the beer batter.
5. Pour vegetable oil into a large skillet to a depth of ½ inch and heat over high heat until hot.
6. Using a skewer, spear each frank and dip it into the batter, letting the excess drip back into the bowl. One at a time, put the franks in the oil, removing the skewer. Cook franks for about 1 minute on each side until golden brown. Lift from the oil with tongs and drain on paper towels. Serve with the sauce on the side.

BLUE CHEESE CRISPS

Makes 12 to 16 servings

1 package (8 oz.) blue cheese, at room temperature	1 tsp. ground white pepper
½ cup unsalted butter, at room temperature	1¾ cups all-purpose flour
1 large egg	¾ cup chopped pecans or hazelnuts

1. In a medium bowl, and using an electric mixer on medium speed, beat together the cheese and butter until smooth. Beat in the egg and pepper. Stir in the flour to make a firm dough.
2. Turn the dough out onto a lightly floured surface and form it into a log about 1½ inches in diameter. Wrap with wax paper and chill for at least 2 hours or until firm.
3. Position the rack in the center of the oven and preheat to 425 degrees.
4. Using a sharp knife, cut the dough into ¼–inch-thick slices and place on an ungreased baking sheet, leaving about 1 inch between each slice. Bake for 8 to 10 minutes, or until lightly browned. Serve immediately.

BLUE CHEESE MUSHROOMS

Makes about 6 servings

1 pound fresh mushrooms, about 1½ inches in diameter
¼ cup sliced green onion
2 tbsp. butter or margarine

1 package (4 oz.) crumbled blue cheese
1 package (3 oz.) cream cheese, at room temperature

1. Position the broiler rack about 6 inches from the heat source and pre-heat the broiler.
2. Remove the stems from the mushrooms and finely chop the stems. Transfer to a skillet, add the onion and butter and cook over medium heat for about 5 minutes until the onions soften. Transfer to a bowl, add the blue cheese and cream cheese and mix well.
3. Spoon the mixture into the mushroom caps, transfer to a broiling pan, stuffed side up, and broil for 2 to 3 minutes or until lightly browned and heated through.

BLUE CHEESE-HAZELNUT SPREAD

Makes 12 to 15 servings

2 packages (8 oz. each) cream cheese, at room temperature
8 oz. blue cheese, crumbled

2 tsp. chopped pimientos
½ cup finely chopped hazelnuts
Cocktail bread or crackers

1. In a bowl, using an electric mixer on medium speed, beat the cream cheese until creamy. Add the blue cheese, pimientos, and hazelnuts and mix well. Cover and chill for at least 24 hours.
2. Remove from the refrigerator at least 1 hour before using. Spread on the bread or crackers.

Cooking note: If packed in a small bowl or jar, this keeps in the refrigerator for up to 10 days.

CANTALOUPE WITH SALMON STRIPS

Makes 24 servings

24 cubes (2½ inches each) cantaloupe

2 tbsp. lime or lemon juice

24 thin strips (3-by-1-inches each) smoked salmon

½ pound seedless green grapes

1. In a bowl, gently toss the cantaloupe with the lime juice to coat.
2. Wrap each melon square with a strip of salmon. Arrange on a tray and garnish with grapes. Cover with plastic wrap and chill for at least 6 hours before serving.

CARROT-AND-DILL QUICHE

Makes 4 to 6 servings

1 prepared unbaked pastry shell
1 large carrot, shredded
4 sliced green onions (green portion only)
2 cups half-and-half
2 tsp. dried dill

4 large eggs
¼ cup grated Cheddar or Wisconsin brick cheese
Drawn Butter Sauce (see page 7)

1. Position the rack in the center of the oven and preheat to 425 degrees.
2. Press the pastry into a 9-inch fluted quiche pan, prick the bottom of the pastry and bake for about 10 minutes, or until the shell starts to harden. Do not let it brown.
3. In a saucepan, combine the carrot, onions, half-and-half and dill and bring to a boil over medium heat. Remove from the heat and cool slightly.
4. Add the eggs 1 at a time, whisking after each addition, and pour the mixture into the pastry shell. Sprinkle the cheese over the top and bake for 25 to 30 minutes or until firm and lightly browned. Cool on a wire rack for about 5 minutes before cutting into wedges and serving with the sauce.

CAVIAR-STUFFED EGGS

Makes 8 servings

4 hard-cooked eggs, cut in half and yolks removed
¼ cup Caviar Spread (recipe follows)

2 drops fresh lemon juice
1 tbsp. minced parsley
Paprika

1. In a small bowl, combine the egg yolks, spread, lemon juice, and parsley.
2. Using a pastry bag fitted with a large fancy tip, press a liberal amount of the filling into each half egg. Sprinkle with paprika and place on a plate, platter, or tray. Chill until ready to serve.

CAVIAR SPREAD

Makes about 1 cup

3 oz. caviar
1 large hard-cooked egg, mashed
¾ cup Italian or vinaigrette salad dressing
1 tbsp. minced white onion
1 tbsp. minced pimiento

In a medium bowl, using a large spoon, blend the ingredients together until well incorporated. Cover and chill for at least an hour.

CELERY-SEED SNACKS

Makes 8 to 10 servings

1 cup all-purpose flour
⅔ cup vegetable shortening
2 packages (3 oz. each) cream cheese

2 tbsp. celery seeds
Celery salt for sprinkling
Curry Dip (recipe follows)

1. Position a rack in the center of the oven and preheat to 375 degrees. Lightly grease a baking sheet.
2. Put the flour in a medium bowl, and using a pastry blender, cut in the shortening and cream cheese to make a soft dough. On a floured work surface, roll the dough to a thickness of ¼ inch. Sprinkle with celery seeds and celery salt. Cut into strips 4 to 6 inches long. Lay the strips on the baking sheet and twist each one.
3. Bake for 4 to 6 minutes or until light golden brown. Transfer to a wire rack to cool slightly and serve with the dip on the side.

CURRY DIP

Makes 1½ cups

1 package (8 oz.) cream cheese
¼ cup sour cream
2 tbsp. chutney
1 tbsp. curry powder
1 tbsp. ginger-flavored brandy

In a blender, combine the ingredients on
medium speed for 12 to 15 seconds or until smooth.
Chill for at least 1 hour before serving.

CHEESE POCKETS

Makes 6 to 8 servings

1½ cups all-purpose flour
¼ cup shelled hazelnuts, chopped fine
¼ cup pecan halves, chopped fine
⅔ cup butter or margarine
3 to 4 tbsp. ice water
2 packages (4½ oz. each) Brie cheese

1. Position the rack in the center of the oven and preheat to 425 degrees. Lightly grease a baking sheet.
2. In a large bowl, combine the flour and chopped nuts. Using a pastry blender, cut in the butter to resemble a coarse meal. Using a large spoon, stir in the water and form the mixture into a soft dough. Divide the dough into quarters and roll each quarter into a 6-inch circle.
3. Place 2 circles on the baking sheet, one package of Brie in the center, and using a pastry brush, moisten the edges of the dough. Place a second dough circle on top of the first and crimp the edges to seal. Repeat with the second package of Brie and remaining dough circles.
4. Bake for 20 to 25 minutes, or until the pastry is a golden brown. Transfer to a wire rack to cool slightly before cutting and serving.

CHEESE PUFFS
Makes 36 puffs

2 cups shredded sharp
  Cheddar cheese
½ cup butter or margarine, at
  room temperature

1 cup all-purpose flour
1 tsp. freeze-dried chives
¼ tsp. salt
Hot Shrimp Dip (recipe follows)

1. Lightly grease a 14-by-12-inch baking sheet.
2. In a medium bowl, using an electric mixer on medium speed, blend
   together the cheese, butter, flour, chives, and salt. Using your hands and
   a spoon, break off pieces of dough and shape into small 1-inch balls,
   placing each ball on the prepared baking sheet. Cover with plastic wrap
   and chill in the refrigerator for 8 to 24 hours.
3. Position the rack in the center of the oven and preheat to 400 degrees.
4. Bake for 15 to 20 minutes, or until they are light golden brown. Serve
   with the dip on the side.

HOT SHRIMP DIP
Makes about 3 cups

2 packages (8 oz. each)
cream cheese, at room
  temperature
8 oz. cooked shrimp,
  chopped

1 red onion, diced
1 tomato, diced
3 small cloves garlic, minced
4 small hot chiles, diced

In the top of a double boiler, combine the ingredients and heat,
stirring until smooth. Pour into a chafing dish and serve hot.

CHEESE
SLICES

Makes 20 servings

½ cup butter or margarine, at
room temperature
2 cups shredded Cheddar
cheese, at room temperature
¼ tsp. Worcestershire sauce
⅛ tsp. cider vinegar

Dash of hot pepper sauce
Salt and pepper
1 cup all-purpose flour
Paprika

1. Position a rack in the center of the oven and preheat to 350 degrees.
   Lightly grease a baking sheet.
2. In a large bowl, combine all of the ingredients except the flour and
   paprika. Add the flour a little at a time to make a dough. Knead lightly and form the dough into a log 1 inch in diameter. Slice the dough
   into ½-inch slices and lay them on the baking sheet about ½-inch
   apart. Bake 12 to 15 minutes or until lightly browned. Sprinkle with
   paprika and transfer to a wire rack to cool. Serve with Hot Mustard
   Sauce (below).

HOT MUSTARD SAUCE

Makes about ⅔ cups

¼ cup red wine vinegar
1 tsp. ketchup
¼ tsp. horseradish
⅓ cup canola oil

1 tbsp. hot dry mustard
2 cloves garlic, minced
salt and pepper

Beat the ingredients together and chill before serving.

CHEESE TRIANGLES

Makes about 48 servings

1 pound grated Monterey
   Jack or Tillamook cheese,
   at room temperature
1 large egg

¼ tsp. salt
½ pound phyllo dough sheets
¼ cup butter or margarine,
   melted

1. Position the rack in the center of the oven and preheat to 400 degrees. Lightly grease several baking sheets.
2. In a medium bowl, combine the cheese, egg, and salt.
3. Unroll the phyllo onto a work surface. Remove 1 sheet and cover the remainder with wax paper and a damp (not wet) towel. Brush the phyllo sheet with melted butter, top with a second sheet and brush it with butter. Cut the sheets into lengthwise strips, about 2 inches wide and about 5 inches long. Spoon 1 tablespoon of the mixture onto one end of the phyllo strip. Fold the corner over to form a triangle and continue folding, as if folding a flag, end over end until you are left with a triangular bundle. Brush the protruding point of dough with butter and tuck into the fold of the triangle to seal. Repeat with remaining phyllo and filling.
4. Place the triangles on baking sheets, leaving about 1 inch between them, and brush with the remaining butter. Bake for 12 to 5 minutes, or until a golden brown and crispy. Serve warm.

CHEESE-FLAVORED PARTY MIX

Makes 10 to 12 servings

3 tbsp. butter or
  margarine, melted
¼ tsp. cayenne
1 tbsp. Worcestershire sauce
½ cup grated Parmesan cheese

2 cups fried potato sticks
2 cans (2.8 oz. each)
  fried onions
2 cups Corn Chex® cereal
1 cup miniature pretzels

1. Position the rack in the center of the oven and preheat to 250 degrees.
2. In a 13-by-9-inch baking pan, combine the butter, cayenne, Worcestershire sauce, and cheese and stir to mix.
3. In a large bowl, toss together the potato sticks, onions, cereal, and pretzels. Add to the baking pan and toss to coat. Bake for 45 minutes, stirring every 15 minutes. Cool slightly in the pan before serving in a festive bowl.

CHEESY TOAST

Makes 6 servings

¾ cup butter or margarine
1 cup shredded Cheddar
  cheese
½ cup shredded mozzarella
  cheese

½ cup grated Parmesan or
  Romano cheese
½ tsp. garlic powder
Pepper
12 thin slices French bread

1. In a bowl, using an electric mixer on medium speed, beat the butter until light and fluffy. Add the cheeses and garlic powder and season with pepper. Spread on both sides of the bread slices.
2. In a nonstick skillet, cook the bread over medium heat for 1 or 2 minutes until browned on the bottom. Turn over and cook the other side until browned. Serve immediately.

CHICKEN-LIVER AND MUSHROOM CUPS

Makes 8 servings

1 package (8 rolls) frozen
  dinner rolls
2 tbsp. butter or
  margarine

½ pound chicken livers
½ cup sliced fresh mushrooms
¼ cup peach-flavored brandy

1. Separate the rolls and press two thin rounds of dough into each cup of a 2½-inch 8-cup muffin tin. Bake as directed on the package.
2. In a small skillet over medium heat, melt the butter. Sauté the livers and mushrooms. Remove from the heat, add the brandy, stir, and spoon into the baked pastry. Serve hot.

CHICKEN WINGS
IN PLUM SAUCE

Makes 15 servings

15 chicken wings
(about 2½ pounds)
Salt and pepper
2 tbsp. peanut
or olive oil
1 small shallot, minced

1 can (8 oz.) crushed pineapple
with juice
⅔ cup plum jam
¼ cup port wine
1 tbsp. soy sauce
1½ tsp. lemon juice
1½ tsp. Dijon mustard

1. Thoroughly wash the chicken wings under running water and cut off
   the tips and discard. Cut the wings at the joints. Season lightly with
   salt and pepper.
2. In a wok or heavy skillet, heat the oil over high heat until very hot and
   stir-fry the chicken wings for 18 to 25 minutes or until golden brown.
3. Drain the pan drippings, add the shallot and stir-fry for about 5 minutes until tender. Add the pineapple and its juice, jam, port, soy
   sauce, lemon juice, and mustard, bring to a boil and cook for about 5
   minutes, or until the sauce reduces by about half and coats the chick-
   en with a pleasing glaze. Serve warm.

CHILI AND NUTS

Makes about 4½ cups

2 tsp. canola oil
1½ cups pecan halves
1½ cups macadamia nuts
1½ cups unsalted almonds
1½ tsp. chili powder

½ tsp. cayenne pepper
¾ tsp. sea salt
½ tsp. sugar
1 tsp. lime juice

1. In a large skillet, warm the oil over medium heat. Add the nuts and cook, stirring frequently, for 6 to 8 minutes until browned. Transfer to a plate.
2. Combine the chili powder, cayenne, sea salt, and sugar and cook in the same skillet over medium heat for a few seconds until fragrant. Add the nuts and toss. Sprinkle the lime juice over the nuts and continue to cook, stirring frequently, until the liquid has evaporated. Drain on paper towels and serve warm.

CHINESE
BEEF KABOBS

Makes about 8 kabobs

2 tbsp. hoisin sauce
1 tbsp. dry sherry
1 tsp. brown sugar
½ tsp. dark sesame oil

8 oz. boneless beef sirloin
    steak, cut into 1-inch cubes
3 green onions, cut into 2-inch
    pieces

1. In a small microwave-safe bowl, combine the hoisin, sherry, sugar, and oil and stir to mix. Microwave on high (100 percent) power for 10 to 15 seconds until hot.
2. In a glass or ceramic bowl, combine the beef and hoisin-sherry sauce, cover and set aside for 1 hour.
3. Thread the meat and onions on skewers. Lay the skewers over a microwave-safe dish and brush with the sauce. Cover with wax paper and cook on medium (50 percent) power for 3 minutes. Turn, brush with the remaining sauce, cover and microwave for 3 to 4 minutes longer, or until cooked through.

CHOPPED BACON-STUFFED EGGS

4 hard-cooked eggs, cut in half and yolks removed
¼ cup Bacon-Endive Sandwich Filling (recipe follows)

¼ cup chopped crisp bacon
Paprika

In a small bowl, combine the egg yolks, filling, and bacon. Using a pastry bag fitted with a large fancy tip, press a generous amount of the filling into each half egg to mound. Sprinkle with paprika and place on a plate, platter, or tray. Chill until ready to serve.

BACON-ENDIVE SANDWICH FILLING
Makes about ½ cup

5 tbsp. finely chopped crisp bacon
3 tbsp. chopped endive
Dash of paprika
2 drops lemon juice

In a small bowl, combine the ingredients and mix with a fork until blended.

CHOPPED
CHICKEN LIVER PÂTÉ

Makes 6 servings

3 cups water
1 pound chicken livers,
  cleaned and trimmed
2 hard-cooked eggs, mashed
  with a fork
1 finely minced large onion
¼ tsp. garlic powder

Salt and pepper
2 tbsp. butter or
  margarine, at room
  temperature
Sprigs of parsley for garnish
Broccoli blossoms for garnish

1. In a medium saucepan over medium heat, bring the water to a boil.
   Add the livers and cook for 5 to 8 minutes, or until no longer pink.
   Drain.
2. Chop the livers and then mash with a fork until smooth. In a large
   bowl, combine the livers, eggs, onions, garlic powder, and season to
   taste with salt and pepper.
3. Add the butter and mash until mixed. Press the mixture into a greased
   3-inch diameter pan, bowl, or ring mold. Cover with plastic wrap and
   chill for at least 4 hours before unmolding. Garnish with parsley and
   broccoli blossoms and serve.

CINNAMON CEREAL
SNACK MIX

Makes 18 to 20 servings

2 cups apple-cinnamon
  flavored cereal
2 cups pecan halves
1 cup whole almonds

1 cup chow mein noodles
2 large egg whites
1 cup sugar

1. Position the rack at the center of the oven and preheat to 350 degrees. Lightly grease a baking sheet.
2. In a large bowl, combine the cereal, pecans, almonds, and noodles and toss. Spread evenly on the baking sheet.
3. Whisk together the egg whites and sugar. Drizzle over the cereal mixture and stir gently. Bake for 40 minutes, stirring frequently to break apart. Transfer to a wax paper-covered work surface and cool completely before serving.

COCKTAIL
CHEESE BALL

Makes about 20 servings

1 cup shredded Cheddar or Colby cheese, at room temperature

2 packages (4 oz. each) blue cheese, crumbled, at room temperature

½ cup Thousand Island dressing

1 large hard-cooked egg, chopped

2 tbsp. diced green bell pepper

2 tsp. Worcestershire sauce

⅛ tsp. hot red-pepper sauce

1 cup chopped pimiento-stuffed olives

Crackers

1. In a bowl, combine the cheeses, dressing, egg, pepper, Worcestershire sauce, and pepper sauce and mash until soft and well mixed. Form into a ball, wrap in plastic and chill for 2 to 3 hours or until firm.

2. Spread the olives in a shallow dish and roll the cheese ball in them to coat. Transfer to a platter and serve with crackers.

COCKTAIL
KABOBS
Makes 24 servings

12 6-inch strips of bacon
24 small raw oysters
24 small shrimp, shelled and
   deveined

24 small white cocktail onions
24 4-inch wooden skewers
Mustard greens for garnish
Creamy Dip (recipe follows)

1. Position the broiler rack 6 inches from the heat and preheat the broiler.
2. Using a sharp knife, cut each strip of bacon into quarters. Thread 1 oyster, 1 shrimp, and 1 onion on each skewer, separating each with a piece of bacon. All of the items on each skewer should be approximately the same size. Repeat with the remaining skewers and ingredients.
3. Lay the skewers on a broiler tray and broil for 3 to 4 minutes. Turn and cook for 2 to 4 minutes more or until the bacon is crisp. Transfer to a serving platter lined with mustard greens and serve Creamy Dip on the side.

CREAMY DIP
Makes 1¼ cup

2 packages (3 oz.) cream cheese, at room temperature
¼ cup heavy cream
2 tsp. snipped fresh chives
¼ tsp. garlic powder
¼ tsp. onion powder
Dash of paprika

In a small bowl, combine the ingredients, whisking until smooth.
Cover and chill for at least 2 hours before serving.

CRAB-AND-AVOCADO FRITTERS

Makes about 48 fritters

1 cup finely diced green onion
1 avocado, finely diced
2 large eggs
½ cup mild salsa
Salt and pepper
2 pounds fresh crabmeat,
    shredded

¼ cup dried bread crumbs
Vegetable oil
All-purpose flour
1 small green bell pepper,
    finely sliced

1. In a bowl, combine the onions and avocado and mix well.
2. In another bowl, combine the eggs and salsa, season with salt and pepper, and stir well. Add the crabmeat and bread crumbs and stir until well mixed. Mix with the avocado mixture.
3. Pinch off pieces of the mixture and form into balls about the size of walnuts and transfer to a baking sheet lined with parchment paper. Cover and chill for at least 4 hours.
4. In a heavy skillet or deep-fat fryer, pour the oil to a depth of 2 inches and heat over medium-high heat until hot (375 degrees in a deep-fat fryer).
5. Spread the flour in a shallow dish and roll the balls in the flour to coat. Fry for 3 or 4 minutes or until golden brown. Drain on paper towels. You will have to cook the fritters in batches. Serve warm, garnished with peppers.

CRAB
CAKES

Makes about 18 servings

1½ cups all-purpose flour
1 cup yellow cornmeal
1 tbsp. plus 2 tsp.
  baking powder
1½ cups milk

2 large eggs, beaten
⅓ cup vegetable oil
2 cans (6 oz. each) crabmeat,
  drained and flaked
Sour cream

1. Preheat a nonstick griddle or large skillet until hot (400 degrees for an electric griddle).
2. In a bowl, combine the flour, cornmeal, and baking powder. Add the milk, eggs, oil, and crabmeat and stir to mix.
3. Drop by ¼-cupfuls onto the griddle and cook for 1 to 2 minutes on each side until browned. Serve hot with the sour cream.

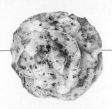

CRABBY
MUFFINS

Makes 8 servings

1 tbsp. butter or margarine
1 cup chopped celery
1 can (10.75 oz.) cream of
   shrimp soup
2 large cans (7.5 oz. each)
   crabmeat, drained and
   flaked

½ cup sour cream and plain
   yogurt
1 tbsp. grated lemon or
   lime zest
Dash of Angostura bitters
4 English muffins, split and
   toasted
Sweet Hungarian paprika

1. In a medium skillet, melt the butter over medium-high heat and sauté
   the celery for about 5 minutes until softened. Add the soup, crabmeat,
   sour cream, lemon zest, and bitters. Stir and heat just to boiling.
2. Spoon over the muffins and serve sprinkled with paprika.

CRISPY
CHICKEN WINGS

Makes 8 servings

12 chicken wings
  (about 2 pounds)
1 large egg
2 tsp. canola oil
2 tsp. soy sauce
1 tsp. sugar
½ tsp. five-spice powder

Salt and pepper
¼ cup sherry
½ cup all-purpose flour
¼ cup cornstarch
½ tsp. baking soda
Vegetable oil

1. Thoroughly wash the chicken wings under running water and cut off
   the tips and discard. Cut the wings at the joints.
2. In a large bowl, combine the egg, canola oil, soy sauce, sugar, and
   spice powder and season with salt and pepper. Add the chicken
   wings, toss to coat, cover, and chill for at least 1 hour.
3. In a small bowl, combine the sherry, flour, cornstarch, and baking
   soda and whisk well. Pour over the chicken and stir gently.
4. In a large skillet or deep-fat fryer, pour oil to a depth of ½ inch and
   heat until hot (350 degrees in a deep-fat fryer).
5. Fry the chicken wings, 5 or 6 at a time, for about 5 minutes, turning
   several times, until nicely browned. Drain on paper towels and fry the
   remaining wings. Serve hot.

CUCUMBER CRAB CAPS

Makes 36 caps

4½ tbsp. mayonnaise
2½ tbsp. fresh lemon juice
5 tsp. Dijon mustard
⅛ tsp. Tabasco sauce
Salt

1 cup shredded cooked
  crabmeat
¼ cup finely chopped celery
1 tbsp. chopped fresh chives
2 cucumbers (each about 6
  inches long)

1. In a medium bowl, using a fork to blend, combine the mayonnaise, lemon juice, mustard and Tabasco sauce. Season to taste with salt. Stir in the crabmeat, celery, and chives. Cover with plastic wrap and chill for 4 hours or overnight.
2. Under running water, thoroughly scrub the cucumbers. Using the tines of a fork, scratch lines on the cucumbers. Chill.
3. Using a sharp knife, slice the cucumber into thirty-six ⅓-inch-thick slices. Arrange the slices on a platter or serving tray and using a teaspoon, top each with crabmeat.

CUCUMBER
STACKS

Makes 6 servings

2 cucumbers
4 oz. sliced smoked salmon
3 or 4 white onions, sliced
⅛ tsp. white pepper

⅛ tsp. garlic powder
Lemon wedges for garnish
Snipped fresh parsley for garnish

1. Using a sharp knife, slice the cucumbers into ¼-inch-thick slices. Using a knife or a round cookie cutter, cut the salmon into circles about the same size as the cucumbers.
2. To assemble, place a slice of salmon on each cucumber slice and top with a slice of onion. Combine the pepper and garlic powder and sprinkle over the salmon. Serve garnished with lemon wedges and parsley.

CURRY-FLAVORED
MEATBALLS

Makes 20 to 32 balls

1 pound lean ground beef
2 tsp. curry powder
1 cup crushed saltine crackers
Salt and pepper

½ cup butter or margarine, at
   room temperature
Broccoli florets for garnish

1. In a large bowl, combine the beef, curry powder, and crackers. Season
to taste with salt and pepper.
2. In a large skillet, melt the butter. Using a melon baller, form the beef
mixture into small balls and cook, turning, for several minutes until
browned. Drain on paper towels. Serve with toothpicks and garnish
with broccoli.

DANISH-STYLE
EGG-AND-SALMON SANDWICHES

Makes 6 servings

3 tbsp. Anchovy Spread with
 Cheese (recipe follows)
6 slices whole-wheat bread
3 to 4 large hard-cooked eggs,
 thinly sliced

12 thin slices smoked salmon
Lemon juice
Snipped chives

Spread the anchovy spread on the bread and arrange a ring of sliced
eggs around the edges. Top with 2 slices of salmon and a sprinkling of
lemon juice. Sprinkle with chives and serve.

ANCHOVY SPREAD
WITH CHEESE

Makes about 1 cup

¾ cup mashed anchovies
2 large hard-cooked eggs, mashed
2 tbsp. grated Parmesan cheese
Dash of cayenne
Heavy cream or evaporated milk

In a bowl, using an electric mixer on medium speed,
blend the anchovies, eggs, cheese, and cayenne until smooth.
Add enough cream to bind. Cover and chill for at least 1 hour.

DEVILED EGGS
WITH OLIVES
Makes 22 servings

11 large hard-cooked eggs
¼ cup mayonnaise
4 tsp. Dijon mustard

1 tbsp. prepared horseradish
½ cup chopped ripe olives
Stuffed Spanish olives, for
  garnish

1. Cut a very small piece from both ends of each egg so it will sit
   upright. Using a crinkle or wavy cutter, make a cut around the middle
   (equator) of the egg. Remove the yolk and reserve the white halves.
2. In a medium bowl, mash the egg yolk, egg white trimmings, mayonnaise, mustard, and horseradish until blended. Stir in the ripe olives.
   Using a pastry bag fitted with a star tip, press the mixture into the
   egg whites. Garnish each with a stuffed olive. Set the eggs on a platter and serve.

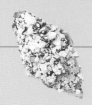

EGG SALAD CANAPÉS
Makes 32 canapés

8 slices whole-wheat bread,
  crusts trimmed
2 tbsp. Mushroom Butter
  (recipe follows)

¾ cup Spinach-and-Egg Filling
  (recipe follows)

1. Using small decorative cookie cutters, cut the bread into various
  shapes, such as hearts, clubs, spades, and diamonds to make 32 pieces.
2. Spread the butter on the bread, spreading it to the edges. Top with a
  layer of filling and serve at once.

MUSHROOM BUTTER
Makes about ½ cup

¼ cup unsalted butter   ¼ cup finely chopped mushrooms

In a small bowl or cup, mash the butter until soft and creamy.
Add the mushrooms and blend thoroughly.

SPINACH-AND-EGG FILLING
Makes about 1½ cup

½ cup chopped fresh spinach
2 tbsp. chopped celery leaves
1 small red onion, diced

4 hard-cooked eggs, mashed
Mayonnaise
Salt and pepper

In a bowl, combine the spinach, celery, onion, and eggs and stir to mix.
Add enough mayonnaise to bind and season to taste
with salt and pepper. Cover and chill for at least 1 hour.

EGG-STUFFED
PIMIENTOS

Makes 8 servings

8 large eggs
8 small whole pimientos,
  peeled and cleaned

Bread crumbs for garnish
Shredded lettuce for garnish

1. Position the rack in the center of the oven and preheat to 350
   degrees. Lightly grease a baking sheet.
2. In a small bowl or cup, beat the eggs individually and pour 1 beaten
   egg into 1 pimiento. Using a toothpick, secure the pimiento closed
   and place on the baking sheet. Bake for about 4 minutes. Sprinkle
   with the bread crumbs and bake until the crumbs begin to brown.
   Cool and slice into 1-inch pieces. Arrange on a bed of shredded lettuce to serve.

Cooking note: Whole pimientos may be difficult to find. Canned pimientos can be used in place of the fresh ones, if necessary.

EMPANADILLOS
DE POLLO

Makes 32 servings

1½ cups finely chopped
cooked chicken
¼ cup Russian dressing
¼ cup chopped toasted hazelnuts or almonds

¼ tsp. crushed red
pepper flakes
2 packages (8 oz. each) refrigerated crescent dinner rolls

1. Position the rack in the center of the oven and preheat to 375
degrees.
2. In a small bowl, combine the chicken, dressing, hazelnuts, and pepper
flakes and stir well.
3. Separate the dough into triangles and lay on a work surface. Cut each
triangle in half and use your hand to flatten slightly. Top each triangle
with about ½ tbsp. of the chicken mixture and fold the dough around
the filling, sealing the edges securely. Transfer to ungreased baking
sheets and bake for 12 to 15 minutes, or until golden brown.

FLAKY SHRIMP BITES

Makes 20 servings

1 package (15 oz.)
 prepared pie crust
20 cooked medium shrimp

¾ cup Dillweed Dip
 (recipe follows)
Lettuce for garnish

1. Position the rack in the center of the oven and preheat to 450
   degrees. Lightly grease a baking sheet.
2. Unwrap the pie crust and cut out as many 3-inch circles as possible.
   Roll out the scraps and continue to cut until all the pastry is used. Dip
   each shrimp in the dip and lay on a circle. Moisten the edges with
   water and fold the dough over, using a fork to crimp and seal the
   edges together. Place on the baking sheet and bake for about 8 to 10
   minutes or until golden brown. Transfer to a plate or platter lined
   with lettuce and serve with the dip on the side.

DILLWEED DIP

Makes about 1½ cups

¾ cup mayonnaise
¾ cup sour cream or plain yogurt
2 tbsp. minced white onions
2½ tsp. snipped fresh dillweed
Salt and pepper

In a small bowl, combine the ingredients and stir until blended. Cover
and chill for at least 2 hours before serving.

FRUIT
ECSTASY

Makes 6 servings

¾ cup crushed pineapple,
   drained
¾ cup fresh raspberries
¾ cup sliced bananas
1 cup diced peaches

1 cup sour cream or berry-
   flavored yogurt
2 tbsp. brown sugar
Pinch of ground cinnamon
Bread or crackers for serving

1. In a large bowl, combine the pineapple, raspberries, bananas, and
   peaches, tossing with a spoon. Cover and chill for 1 hour.
2. In a small bowl, combine the sour cream, brown sugar, and cinnamon,
   beating well with a spoon or fork until the sugar is completely dis-
   solved. Cover and chill for 1 hour.
3. Whisk the chilled sour cream mixture. Add the fruit and fold to incor-
   porate. Transfer to a bowl and set the bowl in a larger one filled with
   ice chips. Serve with the bread or crackers.

FUNGO
ITALIANO

Makes about 24 servings

1 pound large mushrooms, cleaned, stems removed and reserved
¼ cup Italian salad dressing
1 cup fine fresh bread crumbs
¼ cup grated Romano or Parmesan cheese
1 tbsp. finely chopped cilantro (Chinese parsley)

1. Position the rack in the center of the oven and preheat to 350 degrees. Lightly grease a 13-by-9-inch baking dish.
2. Chop the mushroom stems finely and transfer to a bowl. Add the salad dressing, bread crumbs, cheese, and cilantro and stir to mix. Spoon the filling into the mushroom caps, mounding the filling.
3. Place in the baking dish, add water to a depth of ¼ inch, and bake for 18 to 20 minutes, or until the mushrooms are tender.

GREEK
POTATO SKINS

Makes about 24 servings

3 medium-sized baking
  potatoes
4 oz. feta cheese, crumbled
1½ tsp. crushed dried oregano
½ tsp. crushed dried basil

½ tsp. crushed
  dried rosemary
½ tsp. garlic salt
Olive oil

1. Position the rack in the center of the oven and preheat to 400 degrees.
2. Pierce the potatoes in several places with the tines of a fork and bake for 55 to 60 minutes, or until cooked through. Set aside to cool slightly. Raise the oven temperature to 450 degrees.
3. Cut the potatoes lengthwise into quarters and scoop out the potato pulp, leaving a ¼-inch-thick shell. Discard the pulp or reserve it for another use. Cut each quarter into halves and put the skins on an ungreased baking sheet. Bake for about 5 minutes until the skins begin to crisp.
4. In a bowl, combine the cheese, oregano, basil, rosemary, and garlic salt. Spoon the mixture onto the skins and drizzle with olive oil. Bake for 2 or 3 minutes longer until the cheese is bubbly.

Cooking note: The potatoes can be baked several hours ahead of time.

HERBED
CHEESE CANAPÉS
Makes 12 to 14 canapés

½ pound Camembert, at room
temperature
½ cup butter or margarine, at
room temperature
1 tbsp. chopped white onions
½ tsp. anchovy paste
1 tsp. sweet paprika
¾ tsp. crushed caraway seeds
¼ tsp. dry mustard
2 red or green bell peppers,
halved or quartered
6 or 7 thin slices pumpernickel
bread

1. In a bowl, using an electric mixer on medium speed, beat together
the cheese, butter, onions, anchovy paste, paprika, caraway seeds,
and mustard until smooth. Cover and chill for at least 2 hours.
2. Using ½-inch decorative cutters, cut shapes from the peppers, making
sure to cut at least 12 or 14 shapes.
3. Spread the cheese butter on the bread and cut each in half diagonally.
Set a pepper shape in the center of each and serve.

HOT-AND-SPICY
CHICKEN WINGS

Makes 10 to 12 servings

20 chicken wings (about 3
  pounds)
2 tbsp. canola oil
1 can (10 oz.) brown gravy
  with onions

¼ cup ketchup
1½ tsp. hot-pepper sauce
1 tsp. brown sugar
½ tsp. cider vinegar

1. Position the broiler rack 6 inches from the heat and preheat the broiler.
2. Thoroughly wash the chicken wings under running water and cut off
   the tips and discard. Arrange the wings on a broiling pan and brush
   with oil.
3. In a small bowl, combine the gravy, ketchup, hot-pepper sauce, sugar,
   and vinegar and whisk well.
4. Broil the chicken wings for about 15 minutes, or until cooked through,
   turning and brushing several times with the sauce. Serve hot.

LAMB BITES
Makes about 42 servings

1 large egg, beaten
2 tbsp. milk
1 cup fresh breadcrumbs
2 tbsp. finely chopped
  white onion
½ tsp. crushed dried tarragon
1 pound ground lamb

½ cup plain yogurt
¼ cup finely chopped
  cucumbers
1 tbsp. finely chopped
  fresh parsley
Salt and pepper

1. In a bowl, combine the egg, milk, breadcrumbs, onion and tarragon and stir to mix. Add the meat and blend well. Pinch off pieces and form into balls about the size of an unshelled walnut.
2. Put about ⅓ of the meatballs on a microwave-safe dish lined with paper towels and cover with a paper towel. Microwave on high (100%) power for 3 minutes. (If the microwave does not have a turntable, turn the dish once after 2 minutes.) Drain on paper towels and cover to keep warm while cooking remaining meatballs.
3. In a small bowl, combine the yogurt, cucumbers, and parsley and stir to mix. Season to taste with salt and pepper. Serve the meatballs with the yogurt.

LETTUCE
SURPRISE

Makes 8 servings

About 8 soft lettuce leaves
½ cup cooked jasmine rice
¼ cup snipped fresh chives
3 tbsp. sour cream
½ tsp. prepared mustard

½ cup tiny deveined shrimp,
   cleaned and chopped fine
12 thin slices Swiss cheese,
   halved to make strips

1. Thoroughly wash and pat the lettuce leaves dry, lay them between paper towels, and chill for about 1 hour.
2. In a small bowl, combine the rice, chives, sour cream, mustard, and shrimp and stir until well blended. Cover and chill for about 1 hour.
3. Cut the lettuce leaves into twenty-four strips, each about 1 inch wide and 3½ inches long. Avoid the tough whites veins. Lay on a work surface and spoon about ½ teaspoon of the shrimp filling into the center of each. Roll into tight bundles, tucking in the ends.
4. Lay the cheese strips on the work surface and set a lettuce bundle on each. Wrap the cheese around the bundles, tucking in the edges, and chill for about 1 hour. Serve cold.

LITTLE
LINK WRAPS
Makes 24 servings

2 packages (8 oz. each) refrigerated crescent dinner rolls
24 small cooked smoked
sausage links

Ketchup
Prepared horseradish
Prepared mustard

1. Position the rack in the center of the oven and preheat to 375 degrees.
2. Separate the dough into 8 triangles and cut each lengthwise into
   thirds. Lay a sausage on the short end of each triangle.
3. Roll each triangle up to enclose the sausage and place, point side
   down, on an ungreased baking sheet. Bake for 12 to 15 minutes or
   until golden brown. Serve warm with ketchup, horseradish, and
   mustard on the side.

MARINATED
MUSHROOMS

Makes 12 servings

1 pound fresh mushrooms
½ cup virgin olive oil
3 tbsp. lemon or lime juice
1 clove garlic, mashed

⅛ tsp. salt
⅛ tsp. pepper
¼ tsp. crushed dried chervil

1. Using a sharp knife, cut the stems from the mushrooms so that they are even with the bottom of the crown. Gently scrub the mushroom caps with a soft brush or cloth and put in a large jar with a tight-fitting lid. Discard the stems.
2. In a small saucepan, combine the remaining ingredients and bring to a boil over medium-high heat. Immediately pour the hot oil mixture over the mushrooms. Cover loosely and set aside until cool enough to touch. Tighten the cover and invert the jar until cooled to room temperature. When cool, refrigerate for at least 2 days. Turn top to bottom at least twice a day.
3. To serve, drain and serve with toothpicks.

MEXICAN
CHICKEN WINGS

Makes 4 to 6 servings

10 chicken wings (about
  1¾ pounds)
¾ cup biscuit baking mix
2 tbsp. cornmeal
1 tbsp. chili powder

¼ tsp. pepper
¼ tsp. salt
½ cup buttermilk
¼ cup butter or margarine,
  melted

1. Position the rack in the center of the oven and preheat to 425 degrees.
2. Thoroughly wash the chicken wings under running water and cut off
   the tips and discard. Cut the wings at the joints.
3. In a bowl, combine the baking mix, cornmeal, chili powder, pepper, and
   salt. Dip the chicken wings in buttermilk and then coat them with the
   dry ingredients. Place in an ungreased 13-by-9-by-2-inch baking pan and
   drizzle with butter. Bake for 35 to 40 minutes or until lightly browned.

MINIATURE
SMOKED HAM SANDWICHES

Makes 36 servings

2 cups all-purpose flour
1 tbsp. baking powder
1 tbsp. sugar
1 tbsp. light brown sugar
½ tsp. salt
1 cup milk
¼ cup butter, melted
1 large egg

½ cup snipped chives
6 tbsp. butter or margarine,
　at room temperature
6 oz. smoked ham, cut to fit
　the muffins
4 to 5 large hard-cooked eggs,
　thinly sliced
Pepper

1. Position the rack in the center of the oven and preheat to 400 degrees. Lightly grease three 12-cup miniature muffin baking pans.
2. In a bowl, combine the flour, baking powder, sugars, and salt and whisk well. In another bowl, combine the milk, melted butter, and egg and whisk until blended. Add the chives and stir. Pour the wet ingredients into the dry ingredients and stir just until blended.
3. Spoon the batter into the muffin cups, filling each about two-thirds full. Bake for 15 to 18 minutes, or until a golden brown. Turn out onto a wire rack to cool.
4. Halve the muffins crosswise. Spread with butter and fill with 2 to 3 pieces of ham, a slice of egg, and a dash of pepper.

MOROCCAN
EGGPLANT CANAPÉS
Makes 16 canapés

1 to 2 tbsp. butter, melted
16 rye crackers
⅔ cup olive or canola oil
1 small clove garlic, mashed
2 1-pound eggplants, peeled
　and diced
1 onion, chopped
1 package (3 oz.) cream cheese,
　at room temperature

3 tbsp. tarragon vinegar
1 tsp. fresh lemon juice
1 tbsp. snipped fresh chives
Snipped fresh parsley for garnish
Chopped pistachio nuts for
　garnish
Sliced pimiento-stuffed olives
　for garnish

1. In a skillet, heat the oil and garlic over medium heat. Add the eggplant,
   onions, and garlic and cook, stirring, for 12 to 15 minutes until browned.
2. Transfer to a food processor and process until smooth. Add the cheese,
   vinegar, and lemon juice and process until smooth. Transfer to a bowl
   and add the chives. Stir to mix. Cover and chill for at least 24 hours.
3. Brush the butter over the crackers and then spread with a layer of the
   eggplant mixture. Garnish with parsley, nuts, and olives, and serve.

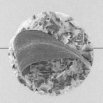

MUSHROOM-GARLIC
ROUNDS

Makes 24 servings

3 slices white bread
3 slices whole-wheat bread
2 tbsp. butter, melted

1 tbsp. butter or margarine
10 mushrooms, finely chopped
½ tsp. garlic powder

1. Preheat the oven to 400 degrees.
2. Using a sharp 1½-inch round cookie cutter, cut each slice of the bread into 4 rounds. Using a pastry brush, lightly coat 1 side of each round with the melted butter. Place the rounds, butter side down, on an ungreased baking sheet and bake for about 5 minutes, or until the bottoms are golden brown. Cool on the baking sheet.
3. In a medium skillet, over low heat, melt the remaining butter and cook the mushrooms for about 5 minutes until lightly browned. Sprinkle with garlic powder and stir until incorporated.
4. Spoon about ½ teaspoon of the mushroom mixture onto the unbuttered sides of the bread rounds, pressing gently with the back of the spoon to cover the rounds. Cover with plastic wrap and refrigerate for 8 to 24 hours. Serve chilled or reheated.

NORTHERN STROMBOLI

About 16 servings

½ loaf (8 oz.) frozen
  bread dough, thawed
¼ tsp. crushed dried oregano
¼ tsp. crushed dried basil
¼ tsp. crushed dried dill

¼ tsp. garlic powder
½ cup shredded Colby or
  Wisconsin brick cheese
¼ cup finely chopped cooked
  ham

1. Position the rack in the center of the oven and preheat to 400 degrees. Lightly grease a baking sheet.
2. On a lightly floured work surface, roll the dough into a rectangle about ¼-inch thick.
3. In a small bowl or cup, combine the oregano, basil, dill, and garlic powder and mix well. Sprinkle over the dough. Sprinkle with cheese and then ham and, starting at a long side, roll into a log, tucking in the edges as you roll. Seal the dough, transfer to the baking sheet and bake for 55 to 60 minutes, or until lightly browned. Cut into slices for serving.

OLIVE AND BACON WRAPS

Makes 8 servings

8 large pimiento-stuffed olives

Cream cheese
8 strips bacon

1. Preheat the broiler.
2. Using a sharp knife, cut the olives in half and place a dab of the cream cheese on 1 half. Rejoin the halves, using the cream cheese as "glue." Wrap each olive with bacon and fasten with a toothpick. Place on a tray and broil for 3 to 4 minutes or until the bacon is crisp. Serve at once.

ONION-AND-MUSHROOM STUFFED EGGS
Makes 8 servings

4 large hard-cooked eggs, cut
    in half and yolks removed

3 tbsp. Mushroom Filling
    (recipe follows)
¼ cup minced white onion
Paprika

In a small bowl, combine the egg yolks, filling, and onion. Using a pastry bag fitted with a large fancy tip, press a generous amount of the filling into each egg white half. Sprinkle with paprika and place on a plate, platter, or tray. Cover and refrigerate until ready to serve.

MUSHROOM FILLING
Makes about 1½ cups

6 tbsp. unsalted butter or margarine
½ cup chopped shallots
16 oz. fresh mushrooms, chopped
2 tbsp. chopped parsley
Salt and pepper

1. In a skillet, melt the butter over medium heat and sauté the shallots for 3 to 4 minutes until translucent. Add the mushrooms and cook for 5 minutes, or until soft and limp. Continue to cook for 5 to 10 minutes, or until most of the liquid evaporates. Reduce the heat to low, add the parsley and cook, stirring, until the mushrooms start to brown.
2. Transfer to a bowl and mash lightly with a fork. Serve warm.

OPEN-FACE
REUBENS
Makes 28 servings

14 slices dark rye bread,
  toasted
Prepared mustard
1 can (16 oz.) sauerkraut,
  drained

6 oz. sliced corned beef,
  chopped
2 cups shredded Leyden or
  Swiss cheese
½ cup mayonnaise

1. Position the rack in the center of the oven and preheat to 375 degrees.
2. Spread the toast with mustard and transfer to an ungreased baking sheet.
3. Put the sauerkraut in a small bowl and use kitchen scissors or two
   sharp knives to cut any long pieces. Add the corned beef, cheese, and
   mayonnaise and mix well.
4. Spread on the toast and bake for about 10 minutes, or until the
   cheese melts. Cut in half on the diagonal and serve hot.

ORIENTAL
STEAK ROLLS
Makes about 24 servings

1 pound sirloin steak	**¼ cup low-sodium soy sauce**
8 green onions	**2 tsp. sugar**
⅓ cup sherry wine	**1 tsp. ground ginger**

1. Position the broiler rack 3 inches from the heat source and preheat the broiler.
2. Using a meat mallet, pound the meat to a thickness of about ⅛ inch. Cut into 4 strips and cut each strip in half. Lay an onion on each strip and, starting at the longest sides, roll the strips around the onions and secure with toothpicks.
3. In a small bowl, combine the sherry, soy sauce, sugar, and ginger and whisk to mix. Lay the steak rolls on a broiler pan and brush with the sauce. Broil for about 3 minutes, turn over, brush again, and broil for 2 to 3 minutes longer, or until cooked through. Remove the toothpicks and cut each roll into 1-inch-long pieces. Serve warm or at room temperature.

ORIENTAL-FLAVORED MEATBALLS

Makes 35 to 40 meatballs

1 pound ground lean pork
¼ cup ground rice cakes
1 large egg
¼ cup milk
2 tbsp. minced onion
3 tbsp. water

Salt and pepper
5 tbsp. butter or
    margarine
1 cup Oriental-Style Dipping
    Sauce (recipe follows)

1. In a large bowl, thoroughly combine the pork, rice cakes, egg, milk, onion, and water. Season to taste with salt and pepper. Using a small melon baller or a spoon, form into small balls.
2. In a large skillet, melt the butter over medium heat. Cook the meatballs for 10 to 12 minutes, turning, until browned on all sides. Drain on paper towels. Serve warm with toothpicks and the sauce on the side.

ORIENTAL-STYLE DIPPING SAUCE

Makes about 1¼ cups

½ cup vegetable oil
¼ cup low-sodium soy sauce
½ cup red wine
3 tsp. sugar

In a small saucepan, combine the ingredients and cook over medium heat, stirring, until the sugar dissolves. Reduce the heat and simmer for 15 to 20 minutes until thickened and the flavors blend. Serve warm.

OYSTER KABOBS

Makes 8 to 10 servings

2 cups finely ground whole-wheat bread crumbs
2 cups finely chopped celery
Salt and pepper
40 canned shucked oysters, drained

3 large eggs, beaten
3 tbsp. butter or margarine, melted
Toast for serving

1. Preheat the broiler.
2. In a small bowl, combine the bread crumbs and celery and season to taste with salt and pepper.
3. Dip the oysters in the egg and then roll in the crumbs until well coated. Thread onto metal skewers, allowing five oysters per skewer. Lay the skewers over a 13-by-9-inch baking pan and brush with melted butter. Broil for 1 to 2 minutes until browned. Turn, brush with butter, and cook the other side until lightly browned. Take care not to overcook. Serve at once with toast.

PEPPER-AND-CHEESE
STUFFED EGGS

Makes 8 servings

4 hard-cooked eggs, cut in
half and yolks removed
¼ cup Cream Cheese Spread
(recipe follows)

2 tbsp. finely chopped green
bell pepper
1 tbsp. finely chopped red bell
pepper
Paprika

In a small bowl, combine the egg yolks, cheese spread, and peppers
and mix well with a fork. Using a pastry bag fitted with a large-sized
fancy tip, press a generous amount of the filling into each egg white.
Sprinkle with paprika and chill until ready to serve.

CREAM CHEESE SPREAD

Makes about 1¾ cups

1 package (3 oz.) cream cheese, softened
½ cup minced pimientos
6 tbsp. mayonnaise
½ cup finely chopped walnuts

1. In a small bowl, using an electric mixer on medium speed, blend
together the cream cheese, pimientos, and mayonnaise.
2. Beat vigorously and stir in the chopped nuts. Cover and chill for at
least 1 hour.

PICKLE
ROLL-UPS

Makes about 48 servings

1 package (8 oz.) cream cheese, at room temperature

1 package (6 oz.) sliced smoked ham
8 medium whole kosher dill pickles

1. Spread 1 tablespoon of the cheese on each slice of ham. Place 1 pickle on the edge of each slice and roll up tight, pressing the edges to seal. Cover and chill for at least 2 hours.
2. Cut each roll-up into 6 equal slices and serve.

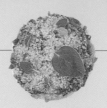

PIZZA BITS

Makes 20 servings

1 package (8 oz.)
  refrigerated biscuits
2 tbsp. butter or margarine
1 clove garlic, minced
1 tbsp. chopped green bell
  pepper
1 tbsp. chopped red bell pepper

⅔ cup tomato sauce
1½ cups chopped cooked
  chicken
2 tbsp. crushed fresh oregano
3 tbsp. grated Parmesan or
  Romano cheese

1. Position the rack in the center of the oven and preheat to 425
   degrees. Lightly grease a baking sheet.
2. Cut each biscuit slice in half and lay the halves on the baking sheet,
   leaving about 1 inch between them.
3. In a skillet over medium heat, melt the butter and sauté the garlic and
   peppers for 5 to 6 minutes until tender. Add the tomato sauce and
   continue cooking, stirring frequently, for about 10 minutes. Remove
   from the heat and stir in the chicken and oregano.
4. Spread the mixture evenly over the biscuit halves and sprinkle with
   cheese. Bake for 8 to 10 minutes, or until the crust starts to turn a
   light brown. Serve hot.

PLUM-AND-CHEESE CANAPÉS

Makes 16 canapés

1¼ cups pitted and coarsely
  chopped fresh plums
1¼ tsp. lemon juice
1¼ packages (8 oz. each)
  cream cheese, at room
  temperature, cut into pieces

⅓ cup plus 2 tbsp. chopped
  pecans
16 small round crackers

1. In a saucepan over low heat, cook the plums, lemon juice and enough water to cover for 5 to 6 minutes, or until the plums are soft.
2. Strain and transfer the plums to a blender or food processor and process on low speed for 5 to 6 seconds. Add the cream cheese and process on low speed for 4 to 5 seconds more, or until smooth. (If using a blender, this may have to be done in batches.) Transfer to a small bowl and stir in ⅓ cup pecans. Cover and chill for at least 3 hours.
3. When ready to serve, spread the crackers with the plum filling and sprinkle with the remaining chopped nuts.

PORK-AND-TURKEY KABOBS

Makes 12 to 16 servings

2 tbsp. minced white onion
¼ cup light soy sauce
¼ cup packed dark brown sugar
¼ cup lemon or lime juice
½ tsp. garlic powder

¾ tsp. ground coriander
⅛ tsp. ground cayenne
2 pounds pork tenderloin, cut into 1-inch pieces
2 pounds boneless turkey roast, cut into 1-inch cubes

1. In the container of a blender, combine the onions, soy sauce, brown sugar, lemon juice, garlic powder, coriander, and cayenne and process until smooth.
2. In a glass or ceramic bowl, combine the pork and turkey, pour the marinade over the meat and toss to coat. Cover and chill for at least 4 hours.
3. Position the broiler rack about 5 inches from the heat source and pre-heat the broiler.
4. Thread the meat on wooden or metal skewers and lay on a broiling pan. Broil for about 8 minutes, turn, and continue broiling for about 8 minutes longer or until browned. Turn again and broil for about 5 more minutes until cooked through. Serve immediately.

Cooking note: If using wooden skewers, soak them in cold water for about 20 minutes to prevent scorching during cooking.

POTATO LATKES
WITH CHIVES

Makes 12 latkes

6 new potatoes, peeled and
cut into 1-inch pieces
1 cup water
1 onion, cut into quarters
2 large eggs, beaten

2 tbsp. snipped chives
1 tbsp. all-purpose flour
½ tsp. salt
½ tsp. paprika
¼ tsp. baking powder

1. Grease a skillet or electric griddle and preheat to hot (400 to 450 degrees).
2. In the container of a blender process half of the potatoes on high speed for 20 seconds, or until finely grated. Transfer to a bowl.
3. Process the remaining potatoes with the water and onions. Add this mixture to the bowl with the grated potatoes. Add the eggs, chives, flour, salt, paprika, and baking powder and mix to make a thick batter.
4. Drop the batter by ¾ cupfuls onto the hot skillet or griddle and cook over medium heat until the edges start to brown. Turn and cook for about 3 minutes longer, or until golden brown. Serve immediately.

PRUNE AND BACON WRAPS

Makes 8 servings

8 large prunes   8 strips bacon
Cream cheese

1. Preheat the broiler.
2. Using a sharp knife, cut the prunes in half and place a dab of cream cheese on 1 half. Rejoin the halves, using the cream cheese as "glue." Wrap each prune with bacon and fasten with a toothpick. Place on a tray and broil for 3 to 4 minutes until the bacon is crisp. Serve at once.

ROMANO
ROUNDS

Makes about 10 servings

⅔ cup grated Romano cheese
½ cup mayonnaise
4 chopped green onions,
  tops only
½ tsp. garlic powder

½ tsp. crumbled dried basil
¼ tsp. crumbled dried oregano
1 package (10 oz.)
  refrigerated biscuits

1. Position the rack in the center of the oven and preheat to 400 degrees.
2. In a bowl, combine the cheese, mayonnaise, onions, garlic powder, basil, and oregano and whisk to blend.
3. Separate the biscuits and lay them on a work surface. Roll out to form circles 5 inches in diameter. Arrange the circles 1 inch apart on ungreased baking pans. Spread 1 tablespoon of the mixture on each circle, leaving ¼-inch border. Bake for 10 to 12 minutes, or until the biscuits are golden brown.

SALMON
CAKES

Makes 4 servings

3 large eggs
2 tbsp. all-purpose flour
2 tsp. lemon or lime juice
2 drops hot-pepper sauce
Salt and pepper

1 can (12 oz.) whole-kernel
 corn, drained
1 can (7 oz.) salmon, drained
 and flaked
Lemon wedges for serving

1. Lightly grease a griddle or skillet and heat until hot.
2. In a bowl, using an electric mixer on high speed, beat the eggs until
   thick and light. Add the flour, lemon juice and hot-pepper sauce and
   season with salt and pepper. Stir in the corn and salmon.
3. Drop the mixture by ½ cupfuls onto the griddle and flatten into a
   patty. Cook for about 3 minutes on each side until golden brown.
   Serve warm with the lemon wedges.

SALMON
CHEESE STRIPS

Makes 48 servings

1 package (3 oz.) cream cheese, at room temperature
2 tbsp. mayonnaise
1 can (7.75 oz.) salmon, finely chopped
½ cup chopped celery

¼ tsp. prepared mustard
Dash of Angostura bitters
16 slices white toast, crusts removed and cut into 1½ - inch strips

In a bowl, combine the cheese and mayonnaise and mash until smooth. Stir in the salmon, celery, mustard, and bitters. Spread on the toast strips and serve.

SALMON PATÉ

Makes 6 to 8 servings

1 can (3.75 oz.) salmon,
   drained and flaked
1 package (8 oz.) cream cheese
¼ tsp. liquid smoke (optional)
2 tbsp. finely chopped green
   onion

1 tbsp. prepared horseradish
1 tbsp. lemon juice
½ cup finely chopped pecans
Parsley for garnish
Crackers

1. In a bowl, using an electric mixer on medium speed, beat the salmon,
   cream cheese, liquid smoke, onions, horseradish, and lemon juice until
   smooth. Form into a log 1½-inches in diameter, wrap in plastic wrap,
   and chill for at least 4 hours or until firm.
2. Unwrap the log and roll it in the pecans to coat. Garnish with parsley
   and serve with crackers.

SALMON QUICHE

Makes 6 to 8 servings

1 can (15 oz.) salmon, drained, cleaned, boned and flaked
4 green onions, sliced
One 9-inch pre-baked pastry shell

3 large eggs
1½ cups light cream
2 tbsp. crushed fresh dill
Salt and pepper

1. Position the rack in the center of the oven and preheat to 375 degrees.
2. In a bowl, combine the salmon and onions and mix well. Spread over the pastry shell and set aside.
3. In the same bowl, using an electric mixer on high speed, beat the eggs until thick and light colored. Add the cream and mix well. Add the dill and season with salt and pepper and mix just to blend. Pour over the salmon and bake for 30 to 35 minutes, or until set and a toothpick inserted in the center comes out clean. Cool slightly on a wire rack and serve cut into wedges.

SALMON ROLLS

Makes 32 rolls

1 can (7.75 oz.) salmon, flaked
1 tsp. prepared horseradish
2 tbsp. lemon or lime juice
1 tsp. finely chopped white
  onion

¼ cup mayonnaise
1 package (11 oz.) pastry pie
  crust mix
Paprika

1. Position the rack in the center of the oven and preheat to 425 degrees.
2. In a medium bowl, combine the salmon, horseradish, lemon juice, onions, and mayonnaise and mix well.
3. Prepare the pastry mix according to the package directions. Divide the dough in half and roll each into a 9-inch diameter circle. Spread the salmon mixture evenly over the two circles and cut each into 16 wedges. Roll each wedge up, beginning at the wide end, and place on an ungreased baking sheet. Prick each roll with the tines of a fork and sprinkle with paprika. Bake for 12 to 15 minutes or until lightly browned. Cool on a wire rack before serving.

SALMON-STUFFED EGGS

Makes 8 servings

8 hard-cooked eggs, cut in half and yolks removed
1 can (3.75 oz.) sockeye red salmon, flaked
½ cup minced celery leaves
½ cup chopped almonds
2 tbsp. minced green bell pepper
¼ tsp. prepared mustard
Mayonnaise
Salt and pepper
Watercress for garnish

1. In a small bowl, combine the egg yolks, salmon, celery leaves, almonds, bell pepper, mustard, and mayonnaise. Season with salt and pepper. Using a fork, mash until smooth.
2. Fill each egg white half with the mixture, garnish with watercress and serve.

SESAME
CHICKEN WINGS

Makes 40 servings

20 chicken wings (about 3
  pounds)
¼ cup plus 2 tbsp. butter or
  margarine, melted
1½ cups biscuit baking mix

½ cup sesame seeds
2 tsp.s paprika
1½ tsp. dry mustard
2 large eggs
2 tbsp. milk

1. Position the rack in the center of the oven and preheat to 425 degrees.
   Spread a 13-by-9-inch baking pan with 1 tablespoon of the butter.
2. Cut the wings at the joints and cut and discard the tips. Toss the
   chicken wings with 2 tablespoons of butter.
3. In a bowl, combine the biscuit mix, sesame seeds, paprika, and mustard and stir.
4. In a small bowl, whisk the eggs and milk until foamy. Dip the chicken
   wings in the egg mixture and roll in the sesame seed mixture. Lay the
   wings on the pan and drizzle with the remaining ¼ cup of butter. Bake
   for 35 to 40 minutes, or until crisp and brown and cooked through.

SOUTHEAST ASIA CRAB ROLLS

Makes about 35 servings

1 can (12 oz.) crabmeat,
   drained and flaked
1 package (8 oz.) cream
   cheese, at room temperature

2 tbsp. grated Romano cheese
¼ tsp. Worcestershire sauce
¼ tsp. garlic powder
1 package egg roll wrappers
Vegetable oil

1. In a bowl, using an electric mixer on low speed, beat together the crabmeat, cream cheese, Romano cheese, Worcestershire sauce, and garlic powder until smooth.
2. Lay about 10 egg roll wrappers on a work surface and spoon tea-spoonfuls of filling into the center or each. Fold into bundles, tucking in the sides and moistening the edges with cold water to seal. Set aside under a damp, well-wrung dishtowel while making the remaining crab rolls.
3. In a large-skillet or deep-fat fryer, pour oil to a depth of 2 inches and heat until hot (350 degrees in a deep-fat fryer).
4. Fry the crab rolls in batches for 3 or 4 minutes on each side until golden brown. Drain on paper towels and set aside, covered, to keep warm while frying the rest of the rolls. Serve immediately.

SOUTHEAST-ASIAN PORK TENDERLOIN

Makes 4 servings

6 Brazil nuts, finely chopped
1 cup minced white onion
2 large cloves garlic, minced
2 tbsp. ground coriander
2 tbsp. brown sugar
¼ cup lemon juice
¼ cup soy sauce
¼ cup olive oil

4 pequin chiles or other hot chiles, crushed
2 pounds pork tenderloin, cut crosswise into 1-inch cubes
Sliced candied kumquats
Orange or lemon leaves for garnish

1. In a large glass or ceramic bowl, combine the nuts, onion, garlic, coriander, brown sugar, lemon juice, soy sauce, olive oil, and chiles and stir to mix. Add the pork and stir to coat. Cover and set aside to marinate for at least 10 minutes.
2. Preheat a stove top grill or prepare a charcoal or gas grill until very hot.
3. Thread the pork on 4 skewers and grill for 10 to 15 minutes, turning and brushing with marinade until cooked through. Serve garnished with kumquats and orange leaves.

Cooking note: If using wooden skewers, soak them in cold water for about 20 minutes to prevent scorching during cooking. If you plan to marinate the meat for longer than 10 minutes, put it in the refrigerator.

SOUTHERN STROMBOLI

Makes 32 serving

1 package (16 oz.) frozen bread dough, thawed	½ pound sliced pepperoni
1 pound sliced boiled ham	3 cups grated mozzarella cheese
½ pound sliced Italian salami	1 can (12 oz.) pizza sauce

1. Position the rack in the center of the oven and preheat to 350 degrees. Lightly grease a baking sheet.
2. Divide the dough in half and roll each into a rectangle about ¼-inch thick. Lay the ham on the rectangles and top with salami and pepperoni.
3. In a bowl, combine the cheese and pizza sauce and drizzle over the meat. Starting at the long sides, roll each into a log, tucking in the edges as you roll. Seal the dough, transfer the logs to the baking sheet and bake for 55 to 60 minutes, or until lightly browned. Cut into slices for serving.

SPANAKOPITA

Makes about 70 servings

12 sheets phyllo dough
½ cup butter or margarine,
  melted
2 packages (12 oz. each) frozen
  spinach soufflé, thawed

6 oz. feta cheese, crumbled
½ cup chopped parsley
½ cup crushed dried dill

1. Position the rack in the center of the oven and preheat to 400 degrees. Lightly grease a 15-by-10-inch baking pan.
2. Bush 6 sheets of the phyllo with butter and fit into the pan, overlapping as necessary. Spread the soufflé over the dough and sprinkle with cheese, parsley, and dill.
3. Brush the remaining 6 sheets of phyllo with butter and lay over the cheese, overlapping as necessary. Score the top into small rectangles and bake for 25 to 30 minutes, or until lightly browned. Cool slightly and cut along the scored lines to serve.

Cooking note: When working with phyllo dough, keep the sheets covered with a damp, well-wrung dishtowel until you are ready to use them to prevent them from drying out.

SPINACH QUICHE

Makes 4 to 6 servings

1 prepared unbaked
  pastry shell
4 tbsp. butter or margarine
2 tbsp. minced green onion,
  white portion only
1 package (10 oz.) frozen
  chopped spinach, cooked
  and drained

1 cup ricotta or cottage cheese
Pinch of ground nutmeg
Salt and pepper
3 large eggs, lightly beaten
½ cup heavy cream
¼ cup shredded Swiss or
  Gouda cheese

1. Position the rack in the center of the oven and preheat to 450
   degrees. Press the pastry into a 9-inch fluted quiche pan, prick the
   bottom of the pastry and bake for about 10 minutes, or until the shell
   starts to harden. Do not let it brown. Reduce the oven temperature to
   375 degrees.
2. Brush the pastry shell with 1 tablespoon of the butter and set aside.
3. In a skillet, melt 2 tablespoons of the butter over medium heat and
   sauté the onions for about 5 minutes until golden brown. Add the
   spinach and cook for about 1 minute. Add the ricotta cheese and
   nutmeg, season with salt and pepper and stir. Add the eggs and
   cream and mix well. Pour into the pastry shell, sprinkle with Swiss
   cheese and dot with the remaining 1 tablespoon of butter. Bake for
   25 to 30 minutes or until set firm.

STUFFED
SHRIMP

Makes 45 to 50 servings

2 tbsp. butter or margarine
⅓ cup finely chopped celery
¼ cup finely chopped onions
1 large clove garlic, minced
1 tsp. crushed dried oregano
1 can (10.75 oz.)
   condensed Manhattan-style
   clam chowder
¼ cup chopped parsley

2 strips crisp-cooked bacon,
   crumbled
⅛ tsp. hot-pepper sauce
1 cup packaged herb-seasoned
   stuffing mix
1½ pounds medium shrimp,
   shelled, deveined, tails intact
Lemon juice

1. Position the broiler rack about 4 inches from the heat source and preheat the broiler.
2. In a saucepan, melt the butter over medium heat and sauté the celery,
   onions, garlic, and oregano for about 5 minutes until the vegetables
   soften. Add the soup, parsley, bacon, and pepper sauce, stir well and
   cook until heated through. Add the stuffing mix and mix well.
   Remove from the heat, cover and let stand for about 5 minutes.
2. Cut each shrimp along the vein line, splitting almost in half, and flatten. Arrange on a broiling pan, brush with lemon juice, and broil for
   about 5 minutes. Spoon 1 tablespoon of the stuffing on each shrimp,
   brush with more lemon juice and broil for about 5 minutes longer or
   until cooked through.

TORTILLA BITES

Makes 72 servings

1 package (8 oz.) cream cheese, at room temperature
1 can (4 oz.) chopped green chiles, drained
1 jar (4 oz.) chopped pimientos, drained

½ cup chopped ripe olives
Twelve 6-inch flour tortillas
About 4 cups tomato salsa (jarred is okay)

1. In a medium bowl, combine the cream cheese, chiles, pimientos and olives and mash with a fork to blend.
2. Spread a heaping tablespoonful of the mixture on each tortilla and roll up tight. Place seam side down, cover, and chill for at least 2 hours. Cut each into 1-inch pieces and serve with the salsa on the side.

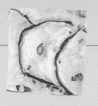

ZUCCHINI SQUARES

Makes about 100 servings

4 cups thinly sliced zucchini
1 cup biscuit baking mix
4 large eggs
½ cup finely chopped
  white onion
½ cup grated Parmesan cheese

½ cup canola oil
2 tbsp. finely chopped parsley
1 small clove garlic, minced
½ tsp. dried oregano, crumbled
Salt and black pepper

1. Position the rack in the center of the oven and preheat to 375 degrees. Lightly grease a 13-by-9-inch baking dish.
2. In a large bowl, combine the zucchini, biscuit mix, eggs, onions, cheese, oil, parsley, garlic, and oregano and stir to mix. Season to taste with salt and pepper.
3. Spread in the prepared baking dish and bake for 25 to 30 minutes until golden brown and a toothpick inserted in the center of the pan comes out clean. Cool slightly, cut into 1-inch squares and serve.